WHO SINGS THE NATION-STATE?

Judith Butler
Gayatri Chakravorty Spivak

WHO SINGS THE NATION-STATE?

language, politics, belonging

LONDON NEW YORK CALCUTTA

Seagull Books 2010

First printed by Seagull Books in 2007
© Seagull Books 2007

PB ISBN   978 1 90649 783 5

British Library Cataloguing-in-Publication Data
A catalogue record for this book is available
from the British Library

Typeset by Seagull Books, Calcutta, India
Printed by Graphic Prints, Calcutta, India

JUDITH BUTLER. Why are we bringing together comparative literature and global states? What are literary scholars doing with global states? We are, of course, caught by the words. What state are we in that we ask these questions about global states? And which states do we mean? States are certain loci of power, but the state is not all that there is of power. The state is not always the nation-state. We have, for instance, non-national states, and

1

we have security states that actively contest the national basis of the state. So, already, the term state can be dissociated from the term "nation" and the two can be cobbled together through a hyphen, but what work does the hyphen do? Does the hyphen finesse the relation that needs to be explained? Does it mark a certain soldering that has taken place historically? Does it suggest a fallibility at the heart of the relation?

The state we are in when we ask this question may or may not have to do with the state we are in. So: how do we understand those sets of conditions and dispositions that account for the "state we are in" (which could, after all, be a state of mind) from the "state" we are in when and if we hold rights of citizenship or when the state functions as the provisional domicile for our work? If we pause for a moment on the meaning of "states" as the "conditions in which we find ourselves," then it seems we reference the moment of writing itself or perhaps even a certain condition of being upset, out of sorts: what kind of state are we in when we start to think about the state?

The state signifies the legal and institutional structures that delimit a certain territory (although not all of those institutional structures belong to the apparatus of the state). Hence, the state is supposed to service the matrix for the obligations and prerogatives of citizenship. It is that which forms the conditions under which we are juridically bound. We might expect that the state presupposes modes of juridical belonging, at least minimally, but since the state can be precisely what expels and suspends modes of legal protection and obligation, the state can put us, some of us, in quite a state. It can signify the source of non-belonging, even produce that non-belonging as a quasi-permanent state. The state then makes us out of sorts, to be sure, if not destitute and enraged. Which is why it makes sense to see that at the core of this "state"—that signifies both juridical and dispositional dimensions of life—is a certain tension produced between modes of being or mental states, temporary or provisional constellations of mind of one kind or another, and juridical and military complexes that govern how and where we may move, associate, work, and speak.

If the state is what "binds," it is also clearly what can and does unbind. And if the state binds in the name of the nation, conjuring a certain version of the nation forcibly, if not powerfully, then it also

unbinds, releases, expels, banishes. If it
does the latter, it is not always through
emancipatory means, i.e. through "letting
go" or "setting free"; it expels precisely
through an exercise of power that depends
upon barriers and prisons and, so, in the
mode of a certain containment. We are not
outside of politics when we are dispossessed
in such ways. Rather, we are deposited in a
dense situation of military power in which
juridical functions become the prerogative
of the military. This is not bare life, but a
particular formation of power and coercion
that is designed to produce and maintain
the condition, the state, of the dispossessed. What does it mean to be at once
contained and dispossessed by the state?
And what does it mean to be uncontained
or discontinued from the state but given
over to other forms of power that may or

may not have state-like features? It won't
do to consider as a kind of stipulative defi-
nition that the refugee belongs to a movement of populations between existing and
autonomous juridical states. When and
where a "refugee" is expelled from one
state, or forcibly dispossessed in some
other way, there is often no place to go,
even as one arrives someplace, if only in
transit. It may be within the borders of a
given state but precisely not as a citizen; so,
one is received, as it were, on the condition
that one does not belong to the set of
juridical obligations and prerogatives that
stipulate citizenship or, if at all, only differ-
entially and selectively. It would seem that
one passes through a border and that one
arrives in another state, but this is where
we do not know whether the state at which
one arrives is defined by its juridical and
military power and its stipulated modes of

national belonging under the rubric of the citizen, or by a certain set of dispositions that characterize the mode of non-belonging as such. And even though one necessarily arrives somewhere (we can see that we are already in a dystopic kind of travel narrative), that is not another nation-state, another mode of belonging; it might be Guantanamo, where there is no state (though delegated state power controls and terrorizes the territory where its inhabitants live), or it might be Gaza, aptly described as "an open-air prison."

The transfer of a population outside the state in such instances is difficult to describe, since it may well be that the transfer or the expulsion founds a state, as took place in the Naqba in 1948. And it may be, as we saw in the cases of Afghanistan and Iraq, that populations were transferred from a state of war, a different kind of state than the one which we conceive as a site of juridical obligation, prerogative, and protection.

The point is to suggest that we cannot presume a movement from an established state to a state of metaphysical abandonment; these movements are more complex and require a different kind of description. Only one of these is described by the act of sovereignty by which constitutional protections are withdrawn and suspended. An abandonment by such protections can happen in different ways, and it is not always possible to suppose that those protections were intact prior to such an abandonment. Moreover, the populations we are trying to describe, those who have become effectively stateless, are still under the control of state power. In this way, they are without legal protection but in no way relegated to a "bare life": this is a life steeped in power. And this reminds us, crucially, that power is not the same as law.

We tend to describe statelessness through certain narrative and tropological procedures. It is, for instance, one thing to be shorn of the political and to be "returned" to a state of Nature (that would constitute yet another sense of what kind of "state" we might be in), but that would be precisely to be without a recognizable location. And though it is sometimes true that arrested and deported populations from the wars in Afghanistan and Iraq are forcibly imprisoned in places where they have not always known where they are, it would be important to distinguish between that imposed and enforced sense of placelessness—an extreme form of dispossession—and the deliberate protocols that establish

and patrol those barriers and cells of the
extra-territorial prison, which are the permutations of state power as it acts outside
the established territorial domain of its sovereignty and, so, materializes sovereignty as
Empire. No one is ever returned to bare
life, no matter how destitute the situation
becomes, because there are a set of powers
that produce and maintain this situation of
destitution, dispossession, and displacement, this very sense of not knowing where
one possibly is and whether there will ever
be any other place to go or be. To say that
the imprisoned are "reduced" to basic ele-
ments is right—that is the published task
and practice of military torture. But it
seems necessary to fathom the paradox
that this reduction and stripping of the
prisoner, especially the prisoner of war, is a
state actively produced, maintained, reiter-
ated, and monitored by a complex and

forcible domain of power, and not exclusively the act of a sovereign or the permutation of sovereign power. After all, the condition of possibility of such extraterritorial prisons is that they escape the *territorial* conditions of sovereignty and constitutionalism as such; or, rather, they are precisely ways of making such claims. And though sovereign-like utterances might justify these institutions by government officials speaking to the media, that is not to say that sovereignty suffices as the full name for the operation of power at work within such prison complexes.

GAYATRI CHAKRAVORTY SPIVAK. You said we're reading Arendt.

BUTLER. Yes, there are surely several relevant distinctions to keep in mind here but the contrast between sovereignty and constitutionalism, even the emergence of

sovereignty in the midst of constitutionalism, is a restrictive conceptualization, one
that casts its "outside" as a metaphysical
state outside of politics itself. This last
move makes use of a certain reading of
Arendt's *Human Condition*, but is it the right
one? And if we seek recourse instead to
"The Decline of the Nation-State and the
End of the Rights of Man," in *The Origins of
Totalitarianism*, are we in a different situation? The category of the stateless is repro-
duced not simply by the nation-state but by
a certain operation of power that seeks to
forcibly align nation with state, one that
takes the hyphen, as it were, as chain. At
least two implications follow: the nation-
state expels and contains those individuals
(whom Arendt consistently regards as
"national minorities") in zones for which
"oversight" is yet another permutation of
the very nation-state in need of monitoring

and intervention, and yet another to be produced as a stateless person contained and
restricted by the juridical and military operations of state power. I don't consider myself
a student or a teacher of globalization, so I
cannot speak very thoughtfully about this
topic. What perhaps I can tentatively broach
is the problem of statelessness.

Arendt is obviously important given the
politicization of immigration rights in the
United States right now, but also for thinking about certain forms of legal dispossess-
sion that have become long-term tactics of
war. Statelessness is also important because
as much as it is increasingly a problem in
the context of contemporary war, it is,
symptomatically, barely legible as an aca-
demic topic in the social sciences right now.
If one asks: who writes on "statelessness"
these days?—the question is hardly under-

stood. In fact, it is generally dismissed as a
trend of the 1980s. It is not that statelessness disappeared but only that we apparently have nothing *interesting* to say about it
any more. One has to wonder about what
"interesting" means in such a context.

I found myself teaching, quite by accident, the 1951 essay by Hannah Arendt
entitled "The Decline of the Nation-State
and the End of the Rights of Man," origi-
nally published in *The Origins of
Totalitarianism*. I must confess at the outset
that I have not lost my ambivalent relationship to Hannah Arendt, an incredible
writer who took many brave and interesting
political positions. I always balked at *The
Human Condition* which established politics
as a public sphere on the basis of the classical Greek city-state and understood that in
the private domain, a *dark* domain by the

way, necessarily *dark*, slaves and children
and the disenfranchised foreigners took
care of the reproduction of material life.
This last sphere is precisely, for her, *not* the
domain of politics. Politics, rather, presupposes and excludes that domain of disen-
franchisement, unpaid labor, and the barely
legible or illegible human. These spectral
humans, deprived of ontological weight
and failing the tests of social intelligibility
required for minimal recognition include
those whose age, gender, race, nationality,
and labor status not only disqualify them
for citizenship but actively "qualify" them
for statelessness. This last notion may well
be significant, since the stateless are not
just stripped of status but accorded a status
and prepared for their dispossession and
displacement; they become stateless
precisely through complying with certain

normative categories. As such, they are *produced* as the stateless at the same time that they are jettisoned from juridical modes of belonging. This is one way of understanding how one can be stateless within the state, as seems clear for those who are incarcerated, enslaved, or residing and laboring illegally. In different ways, they are, significantly, contained within the polis as its interiorized outside.

Arendt's description in *The Human Condition* leaves uncriticized this particular economy in which the public (and the proper sphere of politics) depends essentially upon the non-political or, rather, the explicitly depoliticized, suggesting that only through recourse to another framework of power can we hope to describe the economic injustice and political dispossessions upon which the official polity depends and which it reproduces time and again as part of its efforts at national self-definition. It would seem that this very division is what commands Arendt's discussion when it comes to "statelessness," but it may be that she imagines the stateless primarily through the figure of the refugee, and restricts her understanding of the refugee to that of the exile, one who has left some place and then arrives at another. The idea of passing from one bounded territory to another requires a narrative line in which arrival follows departure and where the dominant themes are assimilation and estrangement.

Surely a certain thematic for comparative literary studies has depended on the legibility of that transition and the stability of those territories that constitute the "then" and "now" as well as the "there" and "here" of emplotment, topology, and narrative line. But I think both spatiality and location have to be reconceived once we consider the departure from within, the dispossession that demands immobility. This seems to be the case for one who is newly, and at once, contained and dispossessed in the very territory from which one both departs and arrives. This would also be true of a corollary type of movement in which one is in a war precisely over a territorial claim, and so the question of "where" one is is already in question, and then one is deported and incarcerated, without ever knowing where one has arrived. There are, doubtless, more permutations of the same, but what this means is that we have to consider the temporal and spatial dimensions of the here and there, the then and now, when it comes to the literature of the stateless, and that these formations establish some distinctive departures from the literature of exile and repression as we have conventionally known it.

Arendt does not offer a critical account of the public/private distinction when she considers the disenfranchised and the stateless. *The Human Condition* postdates *The Origins of Totalitarianism* by about ten years, so one wonders why the analysis in the earlier text does not survive in a more robust form in the later one. In *The Origins of Totalitarianism*, the disenfranchised are clearly national minorities, and the "private" is time and again associated with the interests of capital that come to dominate and eviscerate the public sphere. How do we account for this change in lexicon? In both cases, the economic is rigorously closed off from the public domain of politics, so that in neither case can one introduce a concept such as "economic justice" and

hope to have it make significant sense. Even
though Arendt, for instance, makes clear her
opposition to slavery, she does so not only
or merely on the basis that economic
exploitation is unjust, and not because
innate principles of human dignity were
abrogated. Rather:

> Slavery's fundamental offense
> against human rights was not that it
> took liberty away (which can happen
> in many other situations), but that it
> excluded a certain category of peo-
> ple even from the possibility of
> fighting for freedom—a fight possi-
> ble under tyranny, and even under
> desperate conditions of modern ter-
> ror (but not under any conditions of
> concentration-camp life).[1]

For Arendt, it is important to note that
freedom consists in the exercise of free-

dom; it is something undertaken by a plurality and, hence, a concerted exercise, an
exercise in concert. She refuses both the
natural state of freedom as well as the natural state to which those deprived of freedom are allegedly returned. Nature has
nothing to do with a certain political
mechanism of deprivation that works first
through categorizing those who may or
may not exercise freedom. Power does not
deprive or strip freedom from the person;
freedom establishes those categories of
persons who will be prohibited from the
concerted exercise which, alone, constitutes freedom. The political elaboration
and enforcement of categories thus sup-
plies the "status" for the non-citizen, one
that qualifies the stateless for the deprivation not only of rights of protection but
also of conditions under which freedom

might be exercised. "Qualification" proves to be a juridical procedure through which subjects are both constituted and fore-closed. This bears closer scrutiny on another occasion. And it strikes me as having important links to Gayatri's reflections in "Can the Subaltern Speak?"

I have no doubt that Arendt's criticism of slavery would extend to the descriptions of the non-citizen in classical Athens, but can her call for the public sphere withstand the distinction between public and private that she nevertheless maintains? Can the public ever be constituted as such without some population relegated to the private and, hence, the pre-political, and isn't this radically unacceptable for any radical democratic political vision? Is this very distinction evidence of an anti-democratic ethos in Arendt, one we would have to overcome if we were to extend her reflections on the

stateless more radically and in ways that
speak to contemporary global conditions?
In 1951, she opposed the nation-state for
the ways in which it was bound to expel
and disenfranchise national minorities.
The "public sphere" and the notion of a
"polity" emerge precisely as alternatives to
the "nation-state" and its structural link
with nationalism. But if the public sphere,
ten years later, is elaborated through the
example of classical Athens, has Arendt
simply substituted the class and race politics of classical Athens for the nationalism
of the nation? The public sphere does not
elude the criticisms waged against the
nation-state, though it alters the means
through which statelessness is both
assumed and induced. It is probably
important to note in this regard that,
between the critique of the nation-state and
the defense of the public sphere, Arendt

also seriously considered the rehabilitation of federalism as an alternative polity. She considered it, first, as a way of describing allied efforts to defeat German fascism during the Second World War, then as a possibility for Palestinians and Jews in the mid-1940s, and then in her reconsideration of Madisonian reflections in *On Revolution*. But these thoughts seem to dim by the time *The Human Condition* was written. What is perhaps most interesting about this intermittently sustained recourse to federalism is the critique of sovereignty it was meant to execute. She opposed the federation of sovereign units; she thought that federation could be a way of institutionalizing notions of social plurality that would diffuse sovereignty as well as the prevalent ontologies of individualism. The idea was decidedly non-communitarian as well, since a federation would assume working with

groups with whom there is no necessary
sense of common belonging. Indeed, at its
best, the public sphere meant to do the
same, namely, to oppose the idea that
national modes of belonging supply a legitimating ground for a polity. We govern in
common with those with whom we may
share no sense of belonging at all, and this
refusal to mandate cultural familiarity as
the basis of shared governance was clearly
the lesson to be learned from her critique
of nationalism. It also led her to oppose
the founding of the state of Israel on principles of Jewish sovereignty, a move that
she understood to reignite nationalism and
to perpetuate endless conflict between that
state and those rightful inhabitants of the
lands who were non-Jews.

I confess to maintaining revulsion
against certain dimensions of *The Human
Condition* even as I am taken by Arendt's

notion of action, one that involves words,
speaking, and which makes strong contri-
butions to a notion of politics as performative, as Bonnie Honig's[2] early work clearly
showed. We saw some evidence of how this
works when, earlier, Arendt made clear that
freedom is not a natural capacity that is
deprived in the context of certain social
and political formations; rather, freedom is
an exercise (that exists, then, in the verb
form) and also de-individualized, that is,
an action that takes place in concert (but
which does not presuppose a collective subject). She is trying to make her way through
murky waters here, refusing forms of individualism and collectivity that make her
barely legible on the spectrum of left to
right. My concern is that the elision or
marginalization of the economic or, indeed,
its demonization as a threat to politics as
such, severely restricts this effort to rethink

the terms of concerted action and conditions of statelessness alike. It may be possible to disjoin the account of language as action from the scene in which only the monied and masculine subjects of dominant nationality are entitled to exercise its prerogatives. But it must be possible if we are to retrieve something of Arendt's analysis for thinking through statelessness in the present time. We will return to this problem when we return to consider the enticement of the question: who sings the national anthem?

Arendt is probably one of the first 20th-century political theorists to make a very strong case for performative speech, speech that founds or "enstates" a new possibility for social and political life. What I wish to do is to read her against herself and, perhaps, also suggest that in 1951, only six years after the end of the Second

World War and the liberation of Auschwitz,
she is writing a vexed and complicated text
when she writes *The Origins of
Totalitarianism*. It is a text in which she is
not of one mind, in which she shifts voices
without advance notice. She barely uses the
first-person pronoun in this text; we may
even say that one rhetorical function of the
text is the evacuation of the first-person.
The predominant pronoun that emerges is
a curious "we." Sometimes one has to wonder whether the "we" performs an efface-
ment or perhaps only a displacement, and
where the "I" might be. One goes search-
ing for Arendt in the text that she signs,
but she is not always easy to find. If she is
displaced, this should not be a surprise,
since the topic of this text is the displacement of peoples, and she is writing, as an
exile, in the wake of her own displacement.
The question, "where is she?" is not easily

answerable in this context, nor should it be.
The problem of statelessness is not her
problem (with assistance, she traveled to
France and then to the United States after
an internment at Gurs), nor is it a problem
for European Jewry, but for the political
structure of the nation-state and its particular life in the 20th century (one that would
no doubt start with Russian programs and
the Armenian genocide). The point of her
text is to generalize the problem of statelessness to both political form and historical time and, for this reason, it would
appear that she resists both the pull of
autobiography and of any and all nationalist compensations for geographical and
political displacement.

Arendt refers to statelessness in this
essay, writing in 1951, as the expression of
the 20th century, even as *the political phenomenon* of the 20th century. This is surely

a strong claim. She cannot possibly know,
she has only barely made it into the 51st
year of that century, but, clearly, she is also
saying that whatever else comes next, it will
not deny her thesis. It is an extremely
provocative claim that leaves us, in a way,
to test it or read it and to see in what ways
it remains at all readable for us. Arendt
argues that the nation-state, as a form, that
is, as a state formation, is bound up, as if
structurally, with the recurrent expulsion of
national minorities. In other words, the
nation-state assumes that the nation
expresses a certain national identity, is
founded through the concerted consensus
of a nation, and that a certain correspon-
dence exists between the state and the
nation. The nation, in this view, is singular
and homogeneous, or, at least, it becomes
so in order to comply with the require-
ments of the state. The state derives its

legitimacy from the nation, which means
that those national minorities who do not
qualify for "national belonging" are
regarded as "illegitimate" inhabitants.
Given the complexity and heterogeneity of
modes of national belonging, the nation-
state can only reiterate its own basis for
legitimation by literally producing the
nation that serves as the basis for its legitimation. Here again, let us note that those
modes of national belonging designated by
"the nation" are thoroughly stipulative and
criterial: one is not simply dropped from
the nation; rather, one is found to be wanting and, so, becomes a "wanting one"
through the designation and its implicit
and active criteria. The subsequent status
that confers statelessness on any number of
people becomes the means by which they
are at once discursively constituted within a
field of power and juridically deprived.

The jettisoned life is thus saturated in power, though not with modes of entitlement or obligation. Indeed, the jettisoned life can be juridically saturated without for that reason having rights, and this pertains to prisoners as well as to those who live under occupation. We can, I am sure, think about the circularity of this production in some useful ways, but perhaps at this moment it is enough to remark that to produce the nation that serves as the basis for the nation-state, that nation must be purified of its heterogeneity except in those cases where a certain pluralism allows for the reproduction of homogeneity on another basis. This is, needless to say, not a reason to favor pluralism, but, rather, a reason to be suspicious of any and all forms of national homogeneity, however internally qualified they may be (this would stand as a rebuke as well to efforts to reanimate patriotism on the right and the left).

A fair amount is at stake when we consider how best to think about the nation-state as a political formation that requires periodic expulsion and dispossession of its national minorities in order to gain a legitimating ground for itself. One might think that no nation-state can lay claim to legitimacy if it is structurally and ritually bound up with the expulsion of national minorities. That is doubtless right, but the normative claim that objects to the phenomenon ought not to stop us from understanding the mechanisms through which the phenomenon operates. It matters whether, through such expulsions, the nation-state finds its ground or whether the nation-state (we have to presume there are a number of forms of the nation-state *pace* Arendt's typology) establishes its border, aligning its territory with its assertion of nationality. If the expulsion takes the form of containment, and those expelled minorities are contained within the territory, this differs markedly from those expulsions in which an exterior site contains them, and it matters further whether the exterior site borders on the nation-state's territory. What distinguishes containment from expulsion depends on how the line is drawn between the inside and the outside of the nation-state. On the other hand, both expulsion and containment are mechanisms for the very drawing of that line. The line comes to exist politically at the moment in which someone passes or is refused rights of passage. Further, is it the case that the dispossessed populations are always and only *national* minorities? And what precisely is the mechanism and effect of this dispossession? The nation-state can only put some people, always, in quite a state, but which state is this?

Doubtless, one reason for the rise of interest in Carl Schmitt, perhaps also in Giorgio Agamben's work on this topic, has been the idea that constitutions carry within them the rights of the sovereign to suspend constitutional protections. This runs counter to certain ways of telling the story about the rise of democratic constitutionalism in which sovereignty is overcome through contractarian forms of parliamentary government. In particular, Agamben's reading of the "state of exception" clearly resonates with the operation of power that we have seen in the suspension of constitutional rights to trial and the imprisonment of populations in the name of national security. Indeed, whole wars are waged in the name of national security, a value and an ideal that makes a mockery of any efforts to make the declaration of war contingent upon constitutional or international justifications. The sovereign exercise at issue is one that flouts both kinds of law, even arbitrarily makes up law to suit its needs. It is important to note that Agamben's formulation relies partially on Arendt, though I would suggest that he takes her views in a significantly different direction. In his view, state power understood as sovereign power exercises itself paradigmatically through the capacity to return some part of a population to a state (not a state) that is outside of the polity, one that Agamben, as you know, has described as bare life.[3]

It is not always easy to trace the citational apparatus in Agamben. My best guess is that he put together Arendt's notion of a *bios* that was not yet a *bios politikoon* from *The Human Condition* and, perhaps, also

from "The Decline of the Nation State."
He mentions both in *Homo Sacer* and in
State of Exception. He seems to take the idea
of mere life (*blosses leben*) from Benjamin
who mentions it toward the end of "A
Critique of Violence," but for whom it plays
a role in the early writings from 1918 to
around 1926.

There are many critical questions to be
posed, but one surely has to do with how a
population is cast out of the polis and into
bare life, conceived as an unprotected
exposure to state violence. Can life ever be
considered "bare?" And has not life been
already entered into the political field in
ways that are clearly irreversible? The questions of when and where life begins and
ends, the means and legitimate uses of
reproductive technology, the quarrels over
whether life should be conceived as cell or

tissue, all these are clearly questions of life and questions of power—extensions of bio-power in ways that suggest that no simple exclusionary logic can be set up between life and politics. Or, rather, any effort to establish such an exclusionary logic depends upon the depoliticization of life and, once again, writes out the matters of gender, menial labor, and reproduction from the field of the political. The recourse to Arendt's *The Human Condition* is all the more curious here since it relies on Aris-totle's notions of biology, suggesting not only that contemporary science is irrelevant to the matter of thinking in the sphere of the political but incapacitating any vocabu-lary that might explicitly address all that falls under the rubric of the politics of life.

It may be the case that one crucial and central operation of sovereign power is the capacity to suspend the rights of individu-

als or groups or to cast them out of a polity.
When cast out, one is cast out into a space
or a condition of bare life, and the *bios* of
the person is no longer linked to its political status. By "political" here is meant
membership in the ranks of citizenship.
But does this move not precisely place an
unacceptable juridical restriction on the
political? After all, if to be "bare life" is to
be exposed to power, then power is still on
the outside of that life, however brutally it
imposes itself, and life is metaphysically
still secured from the domain of the political. We can argue that the very problem is
that life has become separated from the
political (i.e. conditions of citizenship), but
that formulation presumes that politics and
life join only and always on the question of
citizenship and, so, restricts the entire
domain of bio-power in which questions of
life and death are determined by other

means. But the most important point here is that we understand the jettisoned life, the one both expelled and contained, as saturated with power precisely at the moment in which it is deprived of citizenship. To describe this doubled sense of the "state" through recourse to a notion of "power" that includes and exceeds the matter of the rights of citizens, and to see how state power instrumentalizes the criteria of citizenship to produce and paralyze a population in its dispossession. This can happen through complex modes of governmentality in ways that are not easily reducible to sovereign acts, and they can happen through modes of instrumentality that are not necessarily initiated or sustained by a sovereign subject. Of course, it is counterintuitive, even exhilarating, to show how sovereignty insists itself in the midst of constitutionalism and at its expense, but it would surely be a mistake if this important way of tracing contemporary power ended up romancing the subject once again. It is one thing to trace the logic of how constitutionalism secures the rights of the sovereign to suspend constitutional protections, but it is quite another to install this logic as the exclusive way in which to apprehend the workings of contemporary power. If our attention is captured by the lure of the arbitrary decisionism of the sovereign, then we risk inscribing that logic as necessary and forgetting what prompted this inquiry to begin with: the massive problem of statelessness and the demand to find postnational forms of political opposition that might begin to address the problem with some efficacy.

The focus on the theoretical apparatus of sovereignty risks impoverishing our conceptual framework and vocabulary so that we become unable to take on the representational challenge of saying what life is like for the deported, what life is like for those who fear deportation, who are deported, what life is like for those who live as *gastarbeiters* in Germany, what life is like for Palestinians who are living under occupation. These are not undifferentiated instances of "bare life" but highly juridified states of dispossession. We need more complex ways of understanding the multivalence and tactics of power to understand forms of resistance, agency, and countermobilization that elude or stall state power. I think we must describe destitution and, indeed, we ought to, but if the language by which we describe that destitution presumes, time and again, that the key terms are sovereignty and bare life, we deprive ourselves of the lexicon we need to understand the other networks of power to which it belongs, or how power is recast in that place or even saturated in that place. It seems to me that we've actually subscribed to a heuristic that only lets us make the same description time and again, which ends up taking on the perspective of sovereignty and reiterating its terms and, frankly, I think nothing could be worse.

You don't disagree so far? You're with me.

SPIVAK. Oh listen, I don't want to say anything more about Agamben because you've already said it but I'm tempted. But you have more, no?

BUTLER. I have more. I'm just going to say a couple things about Arendt's essay. Then I want to talk about what she says about Palestine and about what I think is happening more recently in the United States in terms of the movement for immigrant enfranchisement. Maybe that will lead to a broader discussion.

Excuse my pedagogical excess, but if we return to the Arendt essay, "The Decline of the Nation-State and the End of the Rights of Man," we note that there are two parts; these two parts are written in different voices and there seems to be no easy transition between the partitions operating there. In the first part, Arendt very bitterly, even sardonically, considers whether the *Declaration of the Rights of Man* (1789) really helped anyone in the 19th century or even in the first part of the 20th. Although the doctrine of the rights of man assumed that when and if individuals were returned to a state of Nature they would find their inalienable rights, which would then form the basis of their protection against despotic rule, she criticizes this notion and says that what happens at the moment in which nationalism

takes over a given nation-state—rule of law
is suspended and minorities are deported or
disenfranchised or, indeed, sent off to be
annihilated—is nothing less than the com-
plete destitution of the human as such. This
is a notion of destitution that is without
recourse to any rights at the level of Nature.
Of course, she is right, but my own view is
that she takes the state-of-Nature hypothesis
in Rousseau and others too seriously, that is
to say, too literally. I think there are ways of
understanding the state-of-Nature hypothesis as a kind of fiction that provides a perspective on a given society, perhaps even the
perspective by which a critique of that society
can take place. I'm not sure Rousseau, for
instance, ever thought his state of Nature
existed or should. After all, it only comes
into play once we "set the facts aside."
Importantly, he gives it no place and no
time or he gives it so many places and times

that it becomes impossible to think in terms of stable spatial or temporal coordinates. So it may be that Arendt takes it too literally and it also may be that she has to because she's not just analyzing the intellectual position associated with the state-of-Nature hypothesis but, rather, the historical trajectory and effect of this doctrine when it has been invoked, when people have been deported and/or have lost their rights or been displaced from their homes or have been maintained as second-class citizens vulnerable to state power and without access to any of the rights or entitlements that constitute the prerogatives of citizenship. In a way she's interested in the problem of the discourse of the rights of man in action, whether it has been efficacious, whether it has ever, really, protected anyone.

In the "Decline of the Nation-State" essay, Arendt concludes that this is a weak discourse. You cannot utter it. And if you were to utter it, your utterance could not be efficacious. So the voice that dominates in the first part of the essay is sardonic, skeptical, disillusioned. But in the second half of the essay, she enters into a declarative mode herself. She effectively *redeclares* the rights of man and tries to animate a discourse that she thinks will be politically efficacious. The text is both a critique of (and disdain for) inefficacious discourse, the doctrine of the rights of man, and a new declaration of the rights of man. She says many interesting things about what she thinks humans need in order to survive in their humanness. She says that there are rights to a home and there is a right to rights—a very interesting formulation since that first right cannot be grounded in any established government or social institution; it is not a positive right in that sense.

There also appear to be rights of belonging. There are rights to a social texture of life.

As in the discussion of slavery cited above, there is or, rather, ought to be a right to freedom. It does not exist, but it should, and "declaration" appears to be one of the means by which the right is instanced and exercised. "Declaring" becomes an important rhetorical move-ment, since it is the very freedom of expression for which it calls or, rather, it is the very call of freedom. Freedom cannot pre-exist this call (which is one reason that the appeal to the state of Nature fails), but can only exist in its exercise. Her own dec-laration becomes the exercise of that free-dom, showing what that freedom is or can be. Whether or not that exercise is effica-cious is another matter.

She has a further problem, though, because she wants to hold on to notions of belonging and home. It's 1951. She's been deported twice, from Germany to Paris, and she's in New York. She has arrived somewhere, and she is employed. She knows, of course, of the millions who did not make it, who were not able to get those visas, including her pal Benjamin. Yet there's no "I" here at all. There's no personal testimony, not a moment of personal testimony in the whole text. Perhaps I should not be surprised. She only poses a question: are there modes of belonging that can be rigorously non-nationalist? I think it has to be the case, because the critique of nationalism is so profound, and yet she wants to maintain this right of belonging, at least at this stage in her thinking. What can this right of belonging be? Her critique of the nation-state as a hyphenated reality is so thorough, and she clearly wants a rule of law based on certain kinds of human rights (based upon them or exercising them?) that governs a "polity"—and this word "polity" is precisely the alternative to the nation-state, even if it is based on the classical city-state. But one thing we seem to know is that she does not want that rule of law to be bound by a nation, a national group, a national majority, even a national minority. If the state she wants is a nation-state at all it would be a nation-state that would be rigorously opposed to nationalism and, hence, a nation-state that would have to nullify itself as such. If the community she wants and the modes of belonging she is in favor of are to have any meaning for her in this framework, they would be rigorously non-nationalist. She does not tell us what they might be, but I think she poses that question: what would non-nationalist modes of belonging be? I'm not sure she was describing reality as it is, but making use of language to invoke, incite, and solicit a different future.

I'm going to read you just two more citations from her. She has some strong views about statelessness, and this made her politics nearly illegible in 1951, and before, in 1944 and 1948, when she criticized first forms of political Zionism and then the founding of the state of Israel on the basis of national and religious identity, which, of course, she found illegitimate. She writes:

> The notion that statelessness is primarily a Jewish problem was a pretext used by all governments who tried to settle the problem by ignoring it. None of the statesmen was aware that Hitler's solution of the Jewish problem, first to reduce the German Jews to a nonrecognized

minority in Germany, then to drive
them as stateless people across the
borders, and finally to gather them
back from everywhere in order to
shift them to extermination camps,
was an eloquent demonstration to
the rest of the world how really to
"liquidate" all problems concerning
minorities and the stateless. After
the war it turned out that the Jewish
question, which was considered the
only insoluble one, was indeed
solved—namely, by means of a colonized and then conquered territory
—but this solved neither the problem of the minorities nor the stateless. On the contrary, like virtually
all other events of our century
[again, it's 1951], the solution of the
Jewish question merely produced a
new category of refugees, the Arabs,

thereby increasing the number of
the stateless and rightless by another
700,000 to 800,000 people.

And you'll be interested in this next
moment, Gayatri:

> And what happened in Palestine
> within the smallest territory and in
> terms of hundreds of thousands
> was then repeated in India on a
> large scale involving many millions
> of people. Since the peace treaties
> of 1919 and 1920, the refugees and
> the stateless have attached them-
> selves like a curse to all the newly
> established states on earth which
> were created in the image of the
> nation-state.[4]

SPIVAK. I had a question in the margins:
what does she mean exactly? What happened in Palestine in terms of hundreds of

thousands was repeated in India involving many millions of people?

BUTLER. Well, you would be better equipped than me. But I'm imagining that she was thinking about the population movements that happened as a consequence of independence.

SPIVAK. Partition?

BUTLER. It must be . . .

SPIVAK. Carry on.

BUTLER. I was going to start to tell you about the property laws that were passed in Israel from 1948 to 1953 that institutionalized a certain theft of property in the name of an administrative law, but that will have to wait for another time. Few people really want to hear about that. But, finally, here you see that she actually understands the nation-state as implying statelessness. To have the nation-state is to have statelessness. You might expect that she would counter the critique of statelessness with a call for statehood, but this does not precisely follow. After all, the essay refers to the "the end of the nation-state." And she's declaring it, in some sense. Other words come to take its place, sometimes "federation" and sometimes "polity." The declaring does not make it so, but it is part of the discursive process of beginning something new; it is an inducement, an incitation, a solicitation. There is some wager over whether or not her speech will be efficacious. So then, finally, I want to think about efficacious speech, and how in certain kinds of political speech, assertions and declarations constitute a certain kind of wager.

This has some bearing on the pronouns she uses. She claims that if human beings can act together—something she

theorizes in the context of revolution—
that can happen only by acting together as
a "we." And, in fact, if there is any agency
that is an effective agency, it can only be
the agency of the "we." The text might be
understood to have effected the transformation from "I" to "we," a transformation
that certainly does not suffice as efficacious
action but that constitutes one of its minimally necessary conditions.

She writes, for instance, "Our political
life rests on the assumption that we can
produce equality through organization,
because man can act in and change and
build a common world, together with his
equals and only with his equals."[5] So "man"
here is no individual but a situation of
commonality and equality, both of which
are preconditions of change and building
agency of all kinds. And if this so-called

man is the kind of being who can act and change and build only with his equals, then his individual actions are no good until and unless conditions of equality are established. In other words, her individual action must be an action that is first and foremost an action that seeks to establish equality so that action can become a plural action and, so, stand a chance of becoming politically efficacious.

This notion of man doesn't define a priori features or properties of an individual, but actually designates a relation of equality among beings. This is a kind of ontological claim at the same time that it constitutes a political aspiration (as ontological, it is not for the reason achieved). To give you an understanding of how we could function as a claimant to equality or to the condition of equality, I'm going to turn for a moment to the US national anthem, sung in Spanish. I'm sorry I'm going on too long, but you'll doubtless have a lot of things to say, or so I'm hoping.

SPIVAK. Go on as long as you'd like.

BUTLER. In the last few years, the prospect of rights to legal residency and, ultimately, citizenship have been debated in the US Congress, and time and again we seem to be on the brink of a proposal that will pass. In the spring of 2006, street demonstrations on the part of illegal residents broke out in various California cities, but very dramatically in the Los Angeles area. The US national anthem was sung in Spanish as was the Mexican anthem. The emergence of "*nuestro hymno*" introduced the interesting problem of the plurality of the nation, of the "we" and the "our": to whom does this anthem belong? If we were to ask the question: what makes for a non-nationalist or

counter-nationalist mode of belonging?—
then we must talk about globalization,
something I am counting on Gayatri to do.
The assertion not only claims the anthem,
and so lays claim to rights of possession,
but also to modes of belonging, since who
is included in this "we?" For the "we" to
sing and to be asserted in Spanish surely
does something to our notions of the
nation and to our notions of equality. It's
not just that many people sang together—
which is true—but also that singing is a
plural act, an articulation of plurality. If, as
Bush claimed at the time, the national
anthem can only be sung in English, then
the nation is clearly restricted to a linguistic majority, and language becomes one
way of asserting criterial control over who
belongs and who does not. In Arendt's
terms, this would be the moment when a
national majority seeks to define the nation

on its own terms and even sets up or
polices norms of exclusion deciding who
may exercise freedom, since that exercise
depends upon certain acts of language.
The problem is not just one of inclusion
into an already existing idea of the nation,
but one of equality, without which the "we"
is not speakable. So when we read on the
posters on various public walls that favor
legalization for illegal immigrants—"we are
America"—and we hear illegal immigrants
declaring in the streets, "*il pueblo unido jamás
sera vencido*," we can trace the rhetorical
terms through which the nation is being reit-
erated, but in ways that are not authorized—
or not yet. The monolingual requirement of
the nation surely surfaces in the refusal to
hear the anthem sung in Spanish, but it does
not make the anthem any less sing-able in
that or any other language.

Of course, it is possible to be suspicious of all of this. After all, is it not simply the expression of a new nationalism? Is it a suspect nationalism, or does it actually fracture the "we" in such a way that no single nationalism could take hold on the basis of that fracture? It's an open question to which I don't know the answer. In the middle of this national anthem we hear the words *"somos equales"*: we are equal. One has to pause and wonder: does this speech act—that not only declares boldly the equality of the we but also demands a translation to be understood—not install the task of translation at the heart of the nation? A certain distance or fissure becomes the condition of possibility of equality, which means that equality is not a matter of extending or augmenting the homogeneity of the nation. Of course, this might be no more than a pluralism which, as we know, reinstalls homogeneity only after a little complexity is admitted into the fold. But if we consider this both as plural act and as speech in translation, then it seems to me that we witness at least two conditions that are at work, not only in the assertion of equality but in the exercise of freedom. Both the ontologies of liberal individualism and the ideas of a common language are forfeited in favor of a collectivity that comes to exercise its freedom in a language or a set of languages for which difference and translation are irreducible.

I want to suggest to you that neither Agamben nor Arendt can quite theorize this particular act of singing, and that we have yet to develop the language we need to do so. It would also involve rethinking certain ideas of sensate democracy, of aesthetic articulation within the political sphere, and the relationship between song and what is called the "public." Surely, such singing takes place on the street, but the street is also exposed as a place where those who are not free to amass, freely do so. I want to suggest that this is precisely the kind of performative contradiction that leads not to impasse but to forms of insurgency. For the point is not simply to situate the song on the street, but to expose the street as the site for free assembly. At this point, the song can be understood not only as the expression of freedom or the longing for enfranchisement—though it is, clearly, both those things—but also as restaging the street, enacting freedom of assembly precisely when and where it is explicitly prohibited by law. This is a certain performative politics, to be sure, in which to make the claim to become illegal is precisely what is illegal, and is made nonetheless and precisely in defiance of the law by which recognition is demanded.

Do we conclude that those who claim this, who exercise these rights, who call for and begin to establish the conditions for a certain kind of recognition that depends upon equality, are acting uselessly or cannot be authorized or cannot be recognized? Or do we note that although they have no right under the law to assemble peaceably, because that's one of the rights they'd like to have as citizens, they still do so? They have no right of free speech under the law although they're speaking freely, precisely in order to demand the right to speak freely. They are exercising these rights, which does not mean that they will "get" them. The demand is the incipient moment of the rights claim, its exercise, but not for that reason its efficacity.

Now we can begin to see what Arendt means when she talks about the right to rights. That first right would never be authorized by any state, even as it might be a petition to or for authorization. The second set of rights is the rights that would be authorized by some rule of law of some kind. But it seems to me that the right to rights, emphasizing the first, is one that's not yet guaranteed by the law, but not for that reason "natural" either. Outside all legality, it calls for legal protection and guarantee. So rights we might say exist doubly since there is, on the street and in the song, an exercise of the right to rights, and the first of these rights is guaranteed by no law but belongs to the nature of equality which turns out to be not nature but a social condition. I would even say that it is a state of the social that takes form in discourse and other modes of articulation, including song.

I don't think it would be very easy to imagine Arendt singing and I'm not sure I'd want to. She doesn't have that Nietzschean moment. And I'm not sure I'd want Nietzsche singing either. It would probably still have those Wagnerian undertones. But I confess to liking the singing I heard on the street. That seemed good, that seemed like good singing. I think it leaves us with a question about language, performance, and politics. Once we reject the view that claims that no political position can rest on performative contradiction, and allow the performative function as a claim and an act whose effects unfold in time, then we can actually entertain the opposite thesis, namely, that there can be no radical politics of change without performative contradiction. To exercise a freedom and to assert an equality precisely in relation to an authority that would preclude both is to show how freedom and equality can and must move beyond their positive articulations. The contradiction must be relied upon, exposed, and worked on to move toward something new. There seems to be no other way. I think we can understand it as a mobilization of discourse with some degree of freedom without legal legitimation on the basis of which demands for both equality and freedom are made. But this also involves a deformation of dominant language, and reworking of power, since those who sing are without entitlement. But that does not mean their lives are not mired in power. Obviously, the folks who are singing are not singing from a state of Nature. They're singing from the streets in San Francisco and Los Angeles. And this means that they alter not just the language of the nation but its public space as well. It would finally be an offense to regard it in any other way.

SPIVAK. Finally what?

BUTLER. An offense.

SPIVAK. Yes, a defense, a fantasy.

BUTLER. The call for that exercise of freedom that comes with citizenship is the exercise of that freedom in incipient form: it starts to take what it asks for. We have to understand the public exercise as enacting the freedom it posits, and positing what is not yet there. There's a gap between the exercise and the freedom or the equality that is demanded that is its object, that is its goal. It's not that everything is accomplished through language. No, it is not as if "I can say I'm free and then my performative utterance makes me free." No. But to make the demand on freedom is already to begin its exercise and then to ask for its legitimation is to also announce the gap between its exercise and its realization and to put both into public discourse in a way so that that gap is seen, so that that gap can mobilize.

Even when Bush says, "No, the national anthem can only be sung in English," that means he's already aware that it's not being sung in English and it's already out of his control. He's actually heard the petition and refused it. And, of course, the question that's left is not whether the national anthem should be sung in Spanish. It should be sung in any language anybody wants to sing it in if they want to sing it. And it should emphatically not be sung by anyone who has no inclination to sing it. The question is: is it still an anthem to the nation and can it actually help undo nationalism? And I think that that's an open question for which I don't have the answer.

SPIVAK. No, it's absolutely fascinating. I cite

Kant and you cite Hegel. That's the difference.

BUTLER. Although I've been more interested in Kant recently.

SPIVAK. I remain interested in Hegel, I'm a Marxist. I actually quite like Arendt. Of course, she's not of today. But, on the other hand, she really is trying to come to grips with her situation. There are many things that she talks about which really strike a chord. For example, she sees clearly the fact of many nationalities within a single state. Finally, she talks about the Jews but she really is writing about Eastern and Central Europe. She writes a good deal about Czechoslovakia and the different nationalities within that same state. She sees the state as an abstract structure. When the Spanish national anthem is sung in the streets of San Francisco, the US national anthem in Spanish, that's what she

would be talking about—that the connection between the US state and a putative
American nation (what Samuel Huntington
would call the American Creed) is a historically limited one with a limited future.
What she does not talk about is the
Ottomans when she talks about a state of
many nationalities. As I have written else-
where, when Stalin is giving his speeches
on colonialism he begins before 1917.
Talking to the Bund precisely about different nationalities within the same state, he
says, "Look, we will give you national privileges within the same Soviet state system."
After 1917, it is more an offer of cultural
autonomy. You [Judith] have spoken elo-
quently, with theoretical passion, about the
implications of statelessness in California.
In New York too there is a call for an end
to the idea of illegal aliens through the call
itself. Yet, if we look at the past, we must

notice that, although Arendt mentions the French Revolution, she does not mention the Ottomans. Although she has to record the fact that the number of Armenians is much larger than any of the other numbers that she's dealing with. Her prescience should have taken in conversations taking place today regarding ethnic conflict resolutions in the Caucasus. In Eastern Europe, the memory of the Ottomans is still alive. But Bulgaria, 500 years under Ottoman rule and, strictly speaking, 41 years under Soviet hegemony, is negotiating postcoloniality as postcommunism. The Southern Caucasus today carries the heavy burden of internal displacement (statelessness) and military intervention as a result of the play between the multi-ethnic empires of the Ottoman and the Russians.

I wanted to mark this blind spot before returning to the United States. I agree with Judith strongly that the matter of singing a national anthem does not carry within itself a performative promise of this new thinking of rights to come. What is important to remember, across more or less benign situations, is that the national anthem, incidentally unlike the International (or "We shall overcome"), is in principle untranslatable.

The national anthem of India was written in Bengali, which happens to be my mother tongue and one of the major languages of India. It has to be sung in Hindi without any change in the grammar or vocabulary. It has to be sung in Hindi, because as Bush insists, the national anthem must be sung in the national language. No translation there. When the Indian national anthem is sung, some Bengalis sing loudly with a Bengali pronunciation and accent which is distinctly different from the Hindi pronunciation and accent, but the anthem remains Hindi, although it is Bengali. The nation-state requires the national language.

The anthem mentions many places with different nationalities, different languages, and, sometimes, different alphabets. Two different language families, some of them Indo-European, some Dravidian in structure like the Finno-Ugric agglutinative languages. The anthem also mentions seven religions. Remember, this is not the situation of postcolonial migrations as in Europe or post-Enlightenment immigration as in the United States. These are older formations. Yet, the language of the anthem cannot be negotiated. Arendt theorized statelessness but could not theorize the desire for citizenship.

When Arendt talks about these Eastern European and Central European places, the activities of the Russian and the Habsburg Empires, she tries again and again to say that the minorities were treated as if colonized. This is a good strong point in the context of global states today. If you reterritorialize Hannah Arendt out of the situation in 1951 and the rights of man, you notice arguments that the experiment of the nation-state—suggesting that it is the nation that organizes the modern state—is only slightly more than a century old and has not really succeeded. She says that its disintegration, curiously enough, started at precisely the moment when the right to national self-determination was recognized for all of Europe, and the supremacy of the will of the nation over all legal and abstract institutions—which is the state—was universally accepted. The nation won out over the state, as it were.

Today, it is the decline of the nation-state that we are witnessing in globalization. But the point to be made is that its genealogical force is still strong. In general, the decline is a result of the economic and political restructuring of the state in the interest of global capital. But Arendt allows us to realize that this may also be because the nation-state as a form was faulty from the start. As varieties of nation-state-style unification programs collapse all around us, what is emerging is the old multi-ethnic mix. On the one hand, there are the East and Central European states, the Balkans and the Caucasus. Emergent also are India and China. Huge states with many "nationalities" that cannot be thought of as nation-states in the Arendtian sense. Yet, in spite of the postnational character of global capital, the abstract political structure is still located in the state. The United States has

generated a somewhat postnational com-
bative structure which complicates the
issue.

In such a world, global feminism might
seek to reinvent the state as an abstract
structure with a persistent effort to keep it
clean of nationalisms and fascisms. Indeed,
when you sing the national anthem in
Spanish, it is to these abstract structures
that you are laying claim. As Judith insisted,
the mode of this claim is performative and
utopian. But what utopia does it claim? The
point here is to oppose unregulated capitalism, not to find in an unexamined membership with the capitalist state the lineaments
of utopia. The reinvention of the state goes
beyond the nation-state into critical regionalisms. These polyglot areas and these large
states are of a different model. Hannah
Arendt, speaking of them in the wake of the
Second World War, could only think of it as

a problem. We, in a different conjuncture, can at least think of solutions. It may be possible to redo the fairly recent national boundaries and think about transnational jurisdictions. Conflict resolution without international peacekeeping asks for this precisely in order to fight what has happened under globalization. We think of the decline of the national state as a displacement into the abstract structures of welfare moving toward critical regionalism combating global capitalism. Hannah Arendt thinks of capitalism in terms of class rather than capital. We need a sense of the determining role of something which is neither national nor determined by state. This is capital and Arendt does not think about it.

Let us for a moment consider what globalizing capital does do. Let us also remember that capital's move toward becoming global, which is an inherent characteristic of capital, and which can now happen for technological reasons, is not all related to nation-states or bad politics. Because of this drive, barriers between fragile state economies and international capital are removed. And, therefore, the state loses its redistributive power. The priorities become global rather than related to the state. We now have the managerial state on the free-market model. Galbraith had the sense, a long time ago, to point out to people that the so-called free market was deeply regulated by the interest of capital. When these managerial states with these globally regulated priorities work, some kinds of demands do not come up. The market is never going to throw up demands for clean drinking water for the poor. Other kinds of institutions have to take up these behests away from something

like the state. This discussion would take us
into the international civil society and away
from Arendt. What I am trying to do here
is to sketch the connection between the
global state and Arendt's prescient musings
about the nation-state so we can move
toward what part of the state remains useful. Arendt is writing at the remote begin-
nings of globalization, and is not talking
about capital. Yet, what was happening to
build a new world where statelessness will
become endemic has something rather inti-
mate to do with capital. Ideologically, it was
the beginning of the dismantling of the
welfare state in the north and the dismantling of the developing state in the south.
The World Bank and the International
Monetary Fund began with an international
socialist kind of mission without benefit of
the socialist state structure. If you think of
early projects such as the Indus Valley, you

will see that they were even regionalist in structure. But this phase changed quickly and completely. Development quickly became an alibi for sustainable exploitation. Hannah Arendt reads statelessness as a symptom of the limits of the nation-state. This type of reading is in the tradition of the Eighteenth Brumaire, where Marx reads the bourgeois revolution as the condition of a further consolidation of executive power. Judith has shown us that Arendt stages the stateless as the scene of the rights beyond the nation. It is well known that Marx shows that although the bourgeois revolution seemed to bring in the possibility of parliamentary democracy and citizen participation, what it succeeded in doing was consolidating the power of the executive. Judith speaks of a right inhabiting a performative contradiction. My point would be that those rights that are now in the declarative, in a universal declaration rather than a performative contradiction, are predicated on the failure of both state (Arendt) and revolution (Marx). I have written about this more extensively. To summarize: the imperialism regularized the administration of the colonies, to the extent that they became continuous with the agency of sustained exploitation. The Communist revolutions did the same for another sector. Politics as well as economics nudged the decline of the nation-state. One feature along the way was the old social movements, extra-state collectives working to save civil society from the depradations of the state. What remains of the old impulse now seems increasingly interested in rethinking the state.

Another kind of extra-state collective action entered the global scene after 1989, largely in the interest of sustainable exploitation. The World Trade Organization is its economic arm; the United Nations, the political, and the UDHR, the juridico-legal. This loosely built structure of world governance does not necessarily work in the interests of the states of the global south.

In the global south there already are regional organizations such as the ASEAN and the SAARC. These are basically competitive economic alliances.

What I am speaking of is somewhat different. The question is: in order to win back constitutional redress without ethno-nationalist conflict, what kind of political change do we envisage? The first effort at such cooperation was perhaps at Bandung in 1955 in the name of a Third World. Today, a Bulgarian group is thinking of the structural changes necessary for a critical regionalism. The work of Petia Kabakchieva seems to me of particular interest.

BUTLER. Can we just do a little bit of back and forth here? I just want to ask you a couple questions. Thank you, Gayatri, for reminding us of a couple of things. I guess I want to know a little more about what is meant by critical regionalism. And maybe one of the things that we could both do is to think a little bit about Habermas's efforts to establish democratic politics beyond the nation-state. I think he contin- ues to publish various positions in favor of the European union, suggesting that struc- tures like this can be run democratically, can be models of self-governance that break down nationalisms, and that are postnational. I wouldn't say they're transna- tional. He's aware that the breakdown of the nation-state brings with it neoliberalism

and globalization and inequalities of a new
order at the same time that he seems to
appeal to this notion of democratic
process. It's no accident that he imagines
democratic processes as being able to happen in Europe since Europe has gathered,
according to him, some special capacity to
articulate democratic principles which then
involves not a nationalist assumption but
certainly a cultural assumption and, in fact,
a Eurocentric one, as you say. And I'm just
wondering whether we could think about
the European Union as establishing the self
of self-governance, that is to say the "we"
who governs itself through establishing
borders and immigration policy. And, of
course, one of the bids that the European
Union has made to various countries is:
"Join us and we will help you guard your
borders against unwanted laborers. We will
also make sure that you can get those

cheap laborers and that they'll come in
with less than legal status and with temporary contracts and don't worry, your populations won't alter permanently." Or, "We
could produce a permanent laboring class
for you." But it's not about extending
rights of enfranchisement; it's about the
constitution of a "we" that has internally
porous borders and increasingly rigid
external borders that are, of course, sup-
ported by policy. I'm just wondering what
notion of self-governance this is that can be
housed within the structure that he imagines. And I'm thinking that one could
interestingly contrast the kind of proposal
he makes with what you're calling a critical
regionalism. How would you go about it?

SPIVAK. Critical regionalism is a difficult
thing because of the potency of nationalism, even ethnic sub-nationalism and, on
the other side, because the transnational

agencies go nation-state by nation-state.
But a word first and foremost about
Habermas and the European constitution.
The European constitution is an economic
document. To implement this, a certain
cultural memory is invoked—perhaps to
take the place of mere nationalism. The
treaty toward the European constitution
did not pass because France and the
Netherlands voted "no." The document
begins as if there was always a Europe, even
as people came into it. We know that constitutions must always perform a contradiction, a species of which Judith described.
Yet, there is an asymmetry between different performative contradictions. Thus
Europe bringing itself into being by invoking its originary presence for consolidating
economic unity in the new global market—
and thus giving itself access to cosmopolitheia—cannot be seen as the same as

the undocumented workers in California calling for a right beyond the nation and thus bringing it into being, simply because they inhabit varieties of performative contradiction. When Habermas talks about the advocates of a "cosmopolitan democracy" based in Europe and the creation of a new political status of "world citizens," place it within this argument.

Part of the European dominant's sense of the global is also related to immigration. Here I would like to quote Juan Mosavia, the former director of the International Labor Organization, to which Hannah Arendt also refers. Juan Mosavia was at Davos, the World Economic Forum of 2006, where everybody was emoting over the problem with migrants in Europe. When he was interviewed, he said a small, different, and important thing: he agreed that we ought to be more tolerant, less Eurocentric, that we ought to welcome these immigrants as citizens, etc., going along with the assimilation that was on everyone's agenda, even as it was said that the nationalisms of the immigrants were going to be respected. But he pointed out that we might want to change the politics of our economics. Remember, *Critique of Political Economy* is the sub-title of a famous book. He was smiling, he knew that it was not to be. If, on the other hand, we did do that, and if we emphasized a little local capital as well as global capital, then people may not want to move so much. He was not talking about refugees, he was talking about economics. Let us keep this in mind. Even the rising states in the global south are limiting access to the public sphere for the citizen simply because the state-specific public sphere is shrinking with references to the global economic sphere. There is no robust citizenship for the people down below. These free-market global managerial states are stateless in their own states, if you take the state as an abstract structure. It is that structure of redistribution, welfare, and constitutionality from within the state that's being eroded. When Habermas and other European thinkers talk about cosmopo-litheia, they are talking about Kant. For lack of time, I will merely refer to Derrida's *Rogues* where he attends to the entire Kantian architectonics and shows that Kant's "as if" for thinking the world and freedom and the connection between cos-mopolitheia and war make him unsuitable for thinking and committing oneself to a global democracy to come. And, as I have been insisting, it is not unimportant to look again at Hannah Arendt because, in the context of statelessness, she's thinking the nation and the state separately. Derrida will later call this undoing of the connection between birth and citizenship the decon-struction of genealogy in *Politics of Friendship*. And that is where critical region-alism begins.

In my next book *Other Asias*, I am rec-ognizing, as does everyone, that China, Taiwan, Hong Kong, Indonesia, and other Southeast Asian countries is a region. India and Pakistan, with Sri Lanka, Bangladesh, Sikkim, and Nepal, make South Asia. This region has unilateral connections with China, and Pakistan with West Asia. Japan, as a group of eight states, relates to all of these in still another way. The war in Iraq has involved them in yet another way. Can these regional cross-hatchings happen in a less random way to produce something other than nation-statism, tied by national

sovereignty, to check post-cold war Euro-
US's perennial dream of universalism? I
was recently involved at MOMA with two
radical artists, a woman and a man, from
Iran and Lebanon. Both openly said in
front of an audience, "No, we can't imagine
African Islam." She's speaking about Iran,
he's speaking about Lebanon. Their techniques are so different they can't really talk
to each other. (The Lebanese artist could
talk about his city but not about the possible connections between Iran and
Hizbollah; the Iranian not at all.) Islam has
been deregionalized for a long time and
now especially so on account of the War on
Terror. On the other side is West Asian
nationalism. Iran can historically enter
another West Asian, now Eurasian, regionalist space—the Caucasus and the
Transcaucasus. This is now an important
and fractious region involving Georgia,

Armenia, Azerbaijan, and Chechnya, among others. Old hostilities, pre-dating nation-states, are at play there among more recent ones. NATO is moving in. Oil lines are being policed. Russian and transnational peacekeeping forces are comparing techniques. Here also, "Europe," quite another kind of Europe from Habermas's, is claiming Eurasia. Our global social movements have been taken away from us. We are "helped" at every turn. The lines are not clear. But you do see why the "critical" comes into this thinking of regionalism. In the newspapers, India and Pakistan are still enemies although the prime ministers speak well. China and India are supposedly competing for the favor of the United States. And so on. Do the old lines, pre-dating Bandung, between pan-Africanism and anti-colonialism, survive? Heroes of the humanities like Anyidoho, Ndebele, Ngugi, and Soyinka would make us hope so. Can the New Latin America check the Euro-US craze for universalism? Evo Morales would make us hope so. Hence, why "critical" and why "regionalism." It goes under and over nationalisms but keeps the abstract structures of something like a state. This allows for constitutional redress against the mere vigilance and data-basing of human rights, or public interest litigation in the interest of a public that cannot act for itself.

QUESTION. I have two questions to ask to Spivak. The first question: Paul Gilroy wrote a book called *After Empire* where he put forward the same idea you presented, a cosmopolitan multicultural idea that is beyond the differentiations of race and class in contemporary European society. You also presented the idea of acting and thinking globally. Would you just expand

your idea a little further with a comparison
to Paul Gilroy's idea? This is my first question. My second question is closely related
to Asia. We can say in Asia that India,
China, Taiwan, Hong Kong, and Japan are
different nation-states. Of course, as you
just now elaborated, states are an abstract
entity. Within the boundaries of the nation-
state, there are different kinds of conflicts
and different kinds of yearnings and
beyond these are other different idealiza-
tions. This is just one thing but from another aspect we can say that in history something has been consolidated in East Asia, in
the nation-states I mentioned. The one
thing is Confucianism. Thus, many scholars
have tried to justify the ethical impetus of
modernity in Asia by referring to the impo-
sition of Confucianism. Another is
Buddhism. Buddhism in history comes from

India to China and spreads to other areas in East Asia, including Singapore, Malaysia, Hong Kong, Taiwan, and even Japan. You asked us to think and act globally. A kind of historically particularized something does go beyond something that is regionally and nationally defined already. If we view the whole world as a kind of unity today, then could we idealize something ethically possible, universal, in the contemporary context of globalization? Thank you.

SPIVAK. I think Professor Butler can talk about ethical universalism better than I can. In the context of the global state, I am speaking of political regionalism. I haven't read Paul Gilroy's book yet but I was not actually commenting on cosmopolitanism. I was saying that Habermas and the Europeans talk about cosmopolitan democracy which Derrida questions and I'm influenced by Derrida. I agree with Derrida that the idea of cosmopolitheia will not yield a global democratic future. I was not talking about race and class. I was talking about the abstract structures of the state, as if all redistributive structures could be managed, like getting a driver's license. Getting drivers' licenses is not an epistemic project.

BUTLER. It is if you are an illegal immigrant

SPIVAK. It is a problem, but it's not an epistemic project. It's a juridico-political cut against illegal immigrants, a misuse of nationalism. We want to keep the abstract structures of the states free of the prejudices of nationalism. It's an abstract act, not an epistemic project. Nationalism is an assumption that the epistemic functioning of the national is more in keeping with the state's work and, therefore, more deserving of it. It is not an epistemic project, such as tolerance. The state is a minimal abstract structure which we must protect because it is our ally. It should be the instrument of redistribution. This definitive function has been curtailed in the global state.

With respect, "Asian values" or Confucianism is usually brought up with no discussion of detailed texts, or any expectation of knowledge of language from the other person in order to protect oneself against precisely certain kinds of good demands made by Human Rights Watch, etc. I will not go there. And if you look at the history of classical poetry in China, you will see how hard an apocryphal "Confucianism" tried to curb the freedom of poetic expression by imposing a moral allegory. Capitalism plus Confucianism seems a similar combo. In the history of Buddhism, Gautama Buddha had spoken up *against* the corruption of institutional Hinduism and had the unspeakable courage, 500 years before Christ, to actually produce scriptures in Pali—a creole of Sanskrit. He was a prince and had the rights to the refined language of Sanskrit. Within a hundred years, Buddhism is on the way to becoming an imperial religion. The original Creole Buddhism was defined as Hinayana Buddhism or the lesser vehicle and all the texts were translated into Chinese or Sanskrit. In India, Buddhism has been the refuge of the caste-oppressed. In Myanmar, it has been the vehicle of religious oppression. The fantasmatic "essential" Buddhism celebrated by the Euro-US is a useful piece of cultural history. Islam, which has the greatest internationality— Morocco to Indonesia and beyond—is contaminated by reactive gender politics and "terror." Incidentally, these are international phenomena; "universal" is descriptively wrong; it simply reflects understandably competitive desires. I was therefore not talking about an ethical universalism at all. In his "Religion within the Boundaries of Mere Reason," Kant says that it is not possible to think an ethical *state* as such. I find his analysis convincing. Kant uses the words *gemeines Wesen* over and over again in place of *Staat* (state) in order to make a distinction. In English, the phrase is translated "state," so we lose this important distinction. (Incidentally, a person wrote that by invoking a German original, I was "privatizing" the text. We must remember that English is not the only public language in the world.) I believe you cannot adjudicate an ethical state. Ethics interrupts the abstractions of the state structure. Those structures are legal. They cannot adjudicate justice but they serve justice and we must protect them.

QUESTION. I'm from a political department, and, more specifically, international relations. So a bit of a strategic question. I'm curious about what potentially both of you see in what Derrida alluded to as the strategic potential within sovereign institutions. Pit them against one another? And in the case of critical regionalism, what possibility do you see, in particular as China becomes more open, in something like the International Criminal Court that criminalizes the very concept of sovereignty? How have those tensions and initial resistances played out? What possibilities are there for a politics that is post-sovereign and one that hopes for something administrative beyond the state that is not so restrictive?

BUTLER. I think one perhaps needs to slow down since I'm not sure anybody wants to be *post*-sovereign. The one thing that I had to say about sovereignty is that I think it would be a mistake to take the Schmittian strain in Agamben as the exclusive lens through which one understands the operation of power. I'm trying to open up an analytics of power that would include sovereignty as one of its features but would also be able to talk about the kinds of mobilizations and containments of populations that are not conceptualizable as the acts of a sovereign, and which proceed through different operations of state power. But we could talk about many other analytics as well. Interestingly enough, Arendt says that *the exemplary moment of sovereignty is the act of deportation*. This is very important for us to think about now, given how sovereign power in the US works. Let's remember as well that Bush is, to a certain degree, post-sovereign. In the sense that when the argument was presented that Iraq, whatever its problems, is a sovereign state and on what basis could the US invade it, it was very clear that whatever sovereignty they might have had was illegitimate by virtue of the fact that Bush did not regard that particular government as democratically elected or, even if it were, it was not necessarily legitimate because of its despotic or tyrannical actions. And, of course, that's complicated; the moment this state decides it can invade that one, it exercises a sovereignty that is extra-territorial. So, in our new analytics of power, we are going to have to rethink territoriality and sovereignty alike. Asserting its sovereignty in order to override *that* sovereignty. Then

Guantanamo and apparently various detention centers throughout Europe and Central Asia—the notion of a certain kind of outsourcing of interrogation, imprisonment, torture—which, I think, have to be understood as an exercise of sovereignty outside of the territorial bounds of the US precisely in order to evade the restrictions of habeas corpus but, also, to extend the operation of sovereignty so that it becomes synonymous with Empire. It seems to me that we are seeing new exercises of sovereignty as well as the illegitimacy of the sovereign character of other states as having any kind of final check on US state power. I don't think that the International Criminal Court has criminalized sovereignty but it is true that it wants to develop a set of international protections that are not formulated on the basis of nation-states which is what the Geneva Treaty did. So, part of its promise is to come up with a postnational understanding of what human rights might be. That does not keep that particular mechanism from being taken over by certain states, being run by certain hegemonic interests selectively deciding which kinds of criminal acts it will pursue and which it will not and using all kinds of national and, I would also say, neoliberal criteria in the selection process. Therefore, the point is to be neither pro-sovereign nor to be anti-sovereign but to watch the ways in which sovereignty is invoked, extended, deterritorialized, aggregated, abrogated in the name of sovereignty as well as against the name of sovereignty. A whole map seems to be emerging that's quite important.

BUTLER. I don't know if I can answer your question about the critical possibilities of sovereignty. It does seem to me that the debate on self-determination is important. I'm interested, for instance, in Palestine. We wouldn't know anything about the debates between those who are in favor of self-determination and those who are in favor of a nation-state active in Palestine. Though we see and hear about factional disputes in Palestine between Fatah and Hamas, we are barely ever exposed to the internal political debates among Palestinians. For instance, their one-state or two-state alternatives, the role of violence in political struggle, the contests over territory, the reliability of NGOs or international human rights organizations, the needs for educational and medical infrastructures, how best to preserve them, how to narrate the past, the Naqba in particular, and competing ideas of self-governance and self-determination, to name just a few.

And this situation does not result from the fact that there are just not enough cameras and reporters on the ground. We're committed in advance to a monolithic idea of Palestine, and their "fights" confirm rather than contest a monolithic public idea of who or what Palestine is.

SPIVAK. Proper names. I hear deportation and I also think of Chechnya—the horrible deportation of 1943 and all the different regionalisms tried out with Russia in the 1990s until sovereignty in its crudest understanding brought in unspeakable violence. I hear sovereignty and I think of the Confucianism and Buddhism that was invoked in a previous question.

BUTLER. Unbelievable. I think self-determination is a different notion from nationalism, from the nation-state. Self-determination can sometimes take the form of not calling for the state but for other kinds of regional authorities that would denationalize that territory, so you get some very different kinds of proposals. Self-determination can be a strain of sovereignty; self-legislation can be a strain of sovereignty which is not the same as that operation of sovereignty that deports at will or that withholds rights at will. It seems to be that internally we need to take this concept apart a little more carefully.

SPIVAK. As far as I'm concerned, we can't make a clear-cut distinction between self-determination and nationalism, regionalism and nationalism. There must be a persistent critique that operates during and beyond the rational arrangements. This is the regionalist imperative—discontinuous with the politico-rational. Since national sovereignty is so often misused and Agamben's idea of sovereignty is so remote

from anything that is happening today, we
need to emphasize that what we are talking
about is sovereignty as a negotiable thing.
It is something that is invoked since, strictly
speaking, sovereignty is difficult to practice
today. (Not impossible, however; I am edit-
ing in a tiny rural area where the scion of
the supposedly abolished latifundia system
dispenses change with an unchanging and
fixed ideological authority. Stop press: he
has closed my schools because the students,
graduated into high school, were questioning
authority, in however inchoate a fashion. A
threat to the supposed stasis of sovereignty.)
National sovereignty is indeed sometimes
used in one way but when it is used in
another way, we oppose it. So that the invocation of sovereignty becomes a negotiable
moment that inhabits a field of risk.
Macedonia voted against the International
Criminal Court because Bush promised

recognition of Macedonia as a sovereign republic. I wanted to put on the table the idea of the invocation of sovereignty as a negotiable moment.

QUESTION. I completely agree that we should read the Spanish-language national anthem in the way that you were advancing but I also know that the preponderance of American flags at these demonstrations signify American pride. This is a moment of resurgent nationalism everywhere. For example, I would cite recent European electoral politics, the new fascisms that we face with liberal free-marketeering in Europe. In the Lebanese case, for instance, during the so-called Cedar Revolution, while there was an appeal to the national media network, to Lebanese nationalism and solidarity, the sectarian divides within those crowds were absolutely sharp. How do we pursue the kind of analysis you're

both, I think, advocating, in support of a
critical regionalism? And an attention to
the kind of staking or declaring of a polity
to come or rights to come or rights that are
being exercised and recognized? How do
we negotiate these different analyses of
power that are without Agamben's theory
of sovereignty with the kinds of uncontrol-
lable uses that are made of these national
signifiers again?

BUTLER. Well I mean, with Schwarzenegger,
it's a risk. But I think maybe I see a little
more contingency in it than you do. And I
don't know to what extent the analogy you
offer prefigures your judgment, that this
could only and always be resurgent nationalism. It could be. And, in fact, one of the
frightening things about the enfranchisement movement as it's currently being artic-
ulated is that it could produce 12 million
Republicans. Which I don't think it will. But

there's nothing to keep that from happening. There's no guarantee. I think that we have to ask: why is it that there's nationalist opposition to this particular kind of appropriation of the national anthem and its nationalism? We can say that there's already a fissure at work of some kind. It could be that's all they are wanting: direct assimilation. But it seems to me that there's a critique of the linguistic majority or the idea that the linguistic majority holds or should hold and that's a very different notion of multiculturalism than a singular notion of nation. And I don't know how much of that singing is tactical. I don't know about the people who are not singing but doing some other things and, of course, there is no way to know in advance whether it will be assimilated into what you are calling resurgent nationalism or turn out to be nothing but that or whether it will be mixed up. My

guess is that it's going to be alloyed, that it
will be complex. And, as I understand it, it
is complex already. Some people chose that
anthem as a way to go; there are other people who chose very different ways to go.
The discourse of equality or the discourse
of labor—we are the labor you need, we are
the labor you rely on, watch what happens
to your stores when we don't go to work;
we are part of the system of production and
circulation and distribution and your economy is not functioning without us and that
gives us a certain kind of power—that
strikes me as very different from the
national anthem moment and it may well
be a different kind of we as well. We are the
invisible disenfranchised underpaid labor
that allows your economy to work. So these
are strains in a movement that strikes me
as having potential to moving in several
directions.

QUESTION. About messianism in Arendt and mythopoetics . . . ?

SPIVAK. I found it interesting that you thought Judith was philosophical and I'm practical. Let me say, Dina, that critical regionalism is not an analysis. It is really a kind of fledgling project. It's got a history and it comes, for us, out of experiences such as what happens with the trafficking of women and women living with HIV and AIDS. For Judith, it comes out of the experience of Palestine. The persistent critique might bring in the Gramscian notion of the intellectual being a permanent persuader. It's not an analysis. Obviously, it has its analytical moment. In terms of mythopoetics I'll let Judith answer the question about Arendt, but let me say something that comes very strongly to mind. I'm thinking of people like Simon Gikandi. One of the things Gikandi says is that genocide is often based on narratives. Think of Israel, using an ancient religious narrative. He suggests that because of the destructive potential of a mythopoetic notion of history, he respects written history as a safe thing. Within orality he says it is possible to show that in the narratives themselves there are moments that betray the genocidal version but it is the people within that so-called configuration who have to take an active part in recognizing the active mythopoetic potential of the historical narrative. Not just by citing Herodotus but by taking it as a practical task to come. A mythopoetic notion of history is where history is in the process of becoming. And so it seems to me that one can indeed think of history as mythopoesis in terms of practical politics and not just philosophical speculation, whatever that binary opposition might be. I think it's dangerous in our world to separate the two of them in quite that way. Since you're talking about the Enlightenment, let me mention that Arendt in this essay is ironic about the Kantian moment. In the opening of Kant's "What is Enlightenment?" the concept-metaphor of growing up out of childhood is always translated as "nonage" for some reason. "Independent of the privileges which history had bestowed upon certain strata of society," Arendt writes, "or certain nations, the Declaration indicated man's emancipation from all tutelage and announced that he had now come of age."[6] And indeed that *is* the project of the Enlightenment—making men out of boys. She's ironic here. She's not suggesting that the Declaration has performed the project of the Enlightenment. She mentions the few who have had the advantages. Arendt launches the Enlightenment anew, for what it is worth. The Enlightenment is not something that happens. The Treaty of Westphalia may have "happened" but the Enlightenment as part of that mythopoesis is always belated. We must therefore remember that if we conceive of history as mythopoesis, we must again and again undo the opposition between philosophy and the practical. You cannot say this is not a practical goal and look at me, and say it's a philosophical goal and point at Professor Butler. I'm very serious about this. Because it is . . .

BUTLER. I'm practical . . .

SPIVAK. And I, crudely, vulgarly, against my grain, cannot help being a text of philosophy. I would really urge you to rethink this. I am being a little rude, a little bad form.

And I don't want to dissolve the moment. The world suffers too much from that binary opposition between philosophy and the practical, from banishing history as mythopoesis into the philosophical or the pre-political. Everything suffers.

BUTLER. I wanted to just say one thing which perhaps is obvious but, of course, the idea of critical regionalisms comes out of a very profound and, I think, quite thorough critique of the area studies map and the cold war agenda that spawned the area studies map. So it seems to me that you are remapping a map. I even want to be able to say that that kind of innovation does not come from nowhere. It comes from a history that actually has exercised its violences. The problem with Arendt, now that I have brought her into the discussion, is that when you look, say, at the opening pages of her work on revolution, she imagines a kind of *ex nihilo* beginning. It's an unconditioned coming together of people who then build. And you know they come from places! How did they get there? I think one of the reasons I like this essay is that no one is occupying some ontological condition outside of history and power. If any of these folks are coming together to make a revolution, they're coming together because they've suffered and because they've criticized and because they've bonded together for various reasons and produced solidarity on the basis of an analysis and a history. It seems to me, sometimes, when she uses the notion of self-making as what breaks history, she does it by invoking an unconditioned notion of freedom which, I think, is not really freedom. I accept that there are contingencies, that the Enlightenment does things we didn't expect. That, in the course of history, there are reversals or inadvertent consequences that can be enormously felicitous but I think that's different from going to the notion of a radical *ex nihilo* beginning and, I think, we need to maybe be a little suspect about that.

SPIVAK. In Marx, the revolutionary moment is a moment of false promises. Now that young Euro-US folks want universalism again, I am thinking about this more carefully. Let it remain a cliffhanger, except to say that if Arendt is out of nowhere, *ex nihilo*, Marx is exactly the opposite.

BUTLER. Sorel accepted that from Marx which is why he said we need false pictures of the future in order to mobilize radical strikes and that's right we don't want those to be realized.

So we end here, on the promise of the unrealizable?

Notes

1 Hannah Arendt, *The Origins of Totalitarianism*
   (San Diego, New York & London: Harcourt,
   1994), p. 297.

2 Bonnie Honig, *Political Theory and the
   Displacement of Politics* (Ithaca: Cornell
   University Press, 1993), pp. 96–7, 102–7.

3 Giorgio Agamben, *Homer Sacer: Sovereign
   Power and Bare Life*, tr. Daniel Heller-Rozen
   (Palo Alto: Stanford University Press, 1998),
   pp. 8–10, 148–53.

4 Arendt, *The Origins of Totalitarianism*, pp.
   289–90.

5 Ibid., p. 301.

6 Ibid., p. 290.